Medieval Gower Stories

Ann Marie Thomas

Alina Publishing
Swansea

Published by Alina Publishing
45 Rhondda Street, Mount Pleasant,
Swansea SA1 6ER

ISBN: 978-0-9571988-9-0

Printed by
Kindle Print

Illustrations: Line drawings by Carrie Francis, pictures from Wikimedia & Pixabay and author's own photographs

Also available on Amazon for Kindle and in multiple ebook formats on Smashwords.com, who distribute to major retailers.

Praise for this and other history books:

Ann Marie Thomas has collected together the back story of this tragic figure from Swansea's past. A fascinating account of what really happened in a local landmark many, many years ago...

(Swansea Life magazine)

Though this piece of writing is based on facts, I couldn't help sense a bit of a storyline. Sometimes non fiction can get too caught up in story telling that the underlying facts are put on the backbench but I must stress that while there is an interesting storyline to this piece, the emphasis is on the facts - which is needed in any good non fiction writing. It is a great short piece. The amount of information isn't overwhelming and certainly a good introduction for anybody wanting to research this particular era... it is a wonderful piece that is rich with historical information. It is in fact a great starting point for further research into this field.

(Thomas Falco for Readers Favourite)

We "know" King John. He upset his barons and had to sign Magna Carta. We know little more. This well-written book fills a big hole in history. It explains how their discontent was fuelled by his treatment of the lords of Gower and Swansea. Betrayal and intrigues that make the doings of the Ewings pale into the shade. It is presented in an easy-to-read fashion interesting to young and old. A must-have book.

(Bob Woodward)

Broken Reed: The Lords of Gower and King John reads as easily as any novel of political intrigue. Ann Marie Thomas has a way of telling this tale that captures the reader's emotions and sympathies as much as it relates the facts of this transitional period in history. The well-researched facts are easy to follow and the book will quickly become a page-turner to anyone who is intrigued by the political movements of the nobles of that period. Full of intrigue and a solid piece of historical work, Broken Reed: The Lords of Gower and King John is proof that Ann Marie Thomas has established herself in a role that blends historical fact with a knack for storytelling.

(Bill Howard for Readers Favourite)

About the Author

Writing poetry and making up stories since she was a child, Ann only began to write for publication when her children left home. Her ambition was to write science fiction, but, fascinated by Swansea Castle and distracted by a major stroke she researched local history, an interest that culminated in the publication of her first book *Alina, The White Lady of Oystermouth*, a local history book told as a story, at Easter 2012. Early retirement gave her more time to concentrate on her writing.

The sales of over 300 copies of *Alina* in local shops and museums, and at speaking engagements, led to a second local history book, *Broken Reed: The Lords of Gower and King John* in September 2013, and then to *The Magna Carta Story: The Layman's Guide to Magna Carta* at Easter 2015. The latest book, *Medieval Gower Stories*, is a collection of ten other stories she found in her research, published in October 2017.

During her stroke recovery she wrote poetry, which she published as *My Stroke of Inspiration* in August 2015, a surprisingly cheerful collection. She is still writing science fiction, a series called *Flight of the Kestrel*, and the first book *Intruders* was published in April 2016. The second, *Alien Secrets*, was published in October 2018. The series continues …

Connect with her online:
Website: https://www.annmariethomas.co.uk/
Facebook: http://on.fb.me/1MUd6Kb
Email: amt.tetelestai@gmail.com
LinkedIn: http://linkd.in/1MUdsAv
GoodReads: http://bit.ly/21nG4Jv

FREE BOOK!
Join Ann Marie's mailing list and receive this free book and monthly updates http://eepurl.com/bbOsyz

CONTENTS

Map of Gower

South Wales
11th – 14th
Abergavenny Castle
Brecon
Caerphilly Castle
Dinefwr Castle
Llandeilo
Carmarthen
Kidwelly Castle
Swansea
Neath Abbey
Gower
Gower
Lougher Castle
Swansea Castle
Carngoch Common
Fabians Bay
Swansea Bay
Parc le Breos
Oystermouth Castle
Pennard Castle
Penrice Castle
Llanrhidian Castle

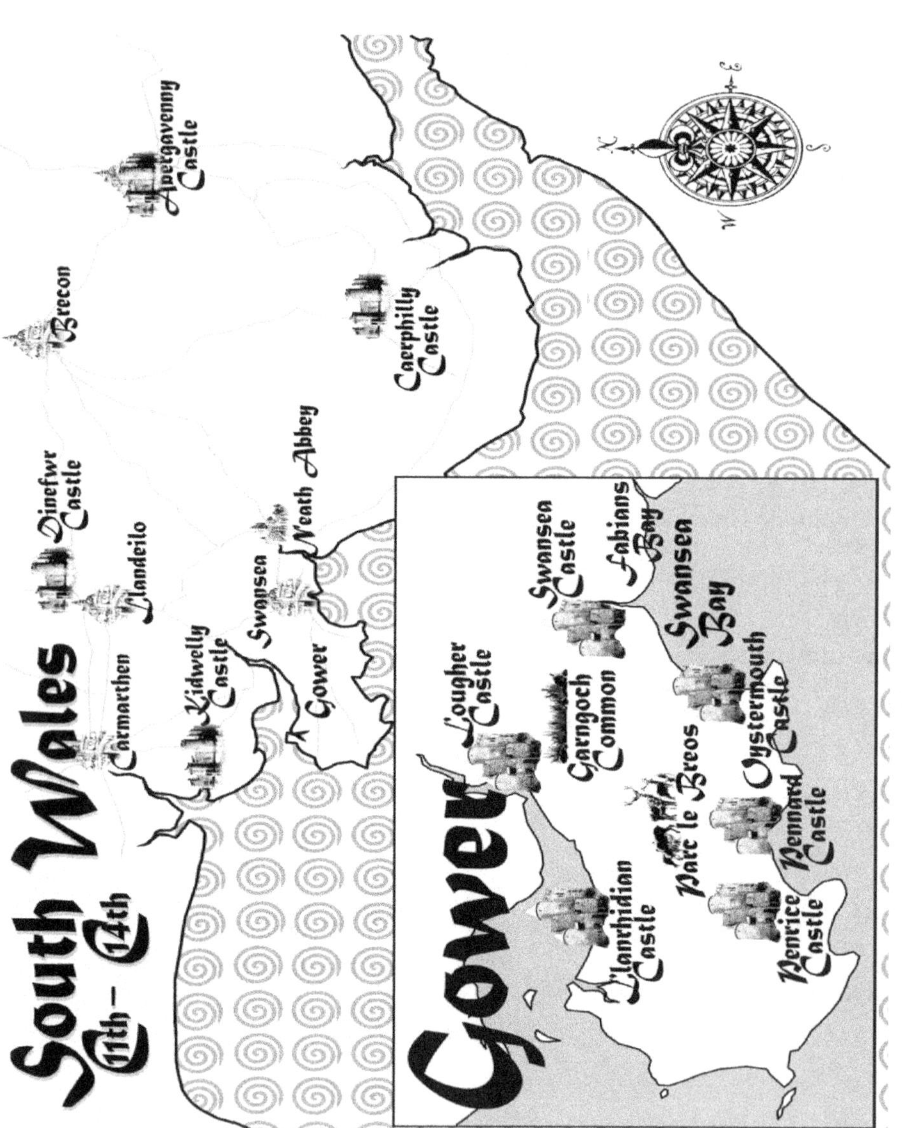

De Braose Family Tree [story numbers in square brackets]

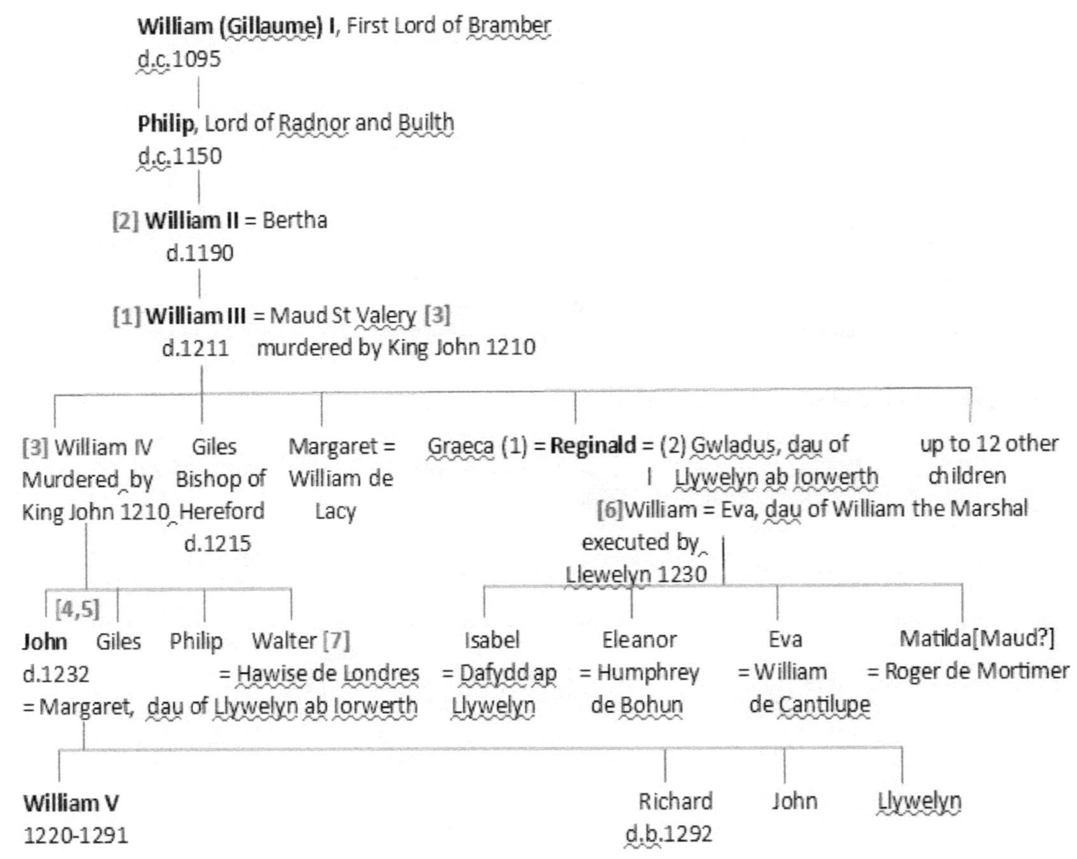

William V
1220-1291
= (1) Alina, dau of Thomas de Multon, Lord of Gilsland
    = Agnes, dau of Nicholas de Moeles
        = Mary, dau of Robert de Ros

Richard
d.b.1292
= Alice le Rus

John

Llywelyn

Giles of Knolton & Woodlands

Richard   Peter   Margaret   William   dau?
of Tetbury   of Tetbury

William VI = (1) Agnes = (2) Elizabeth de Sully m. 1317
1261-1326   d.bfr. 1317

Roger, 1st Baron de Mowbray d.1297

William   Joan = (1) James de Bohun   **Alina** = (1) John de Mowbray 1286-1322 [8]
Lord of Llandimor   d.1323 m.1295 of Midhurst d.1306   1291-1331   m.1298
d. 1320   = (2) Richard Foliot of   = (2) Richard de Peshale [10]
                                   Gressenhall (Norfolk)   **John de Mowbray**   m.1327
                                   d.1317   1310-1361

Hammond = Alice   Walter   Nicholas   Margaret
daughter of Robert de Harley   = Hugh Maleth
                                                                              of Bucks

Introduction

Swansea Castle

I live in the city of Swansea in South Wales UK, right on the edge of the Gower peninsular, Britain's first Area of Outstanding Natural Beauty. We have everything, all in one place: chain stores, little independent shops, leisure centres, museums, theatres, art galleries, the beach, the countryside, and train and motorway links directly to London and lots of other places.

In the past, Swansea was known as Copperopolis, the industrial centre of the world for smelting copper and other metals, due to the close proximity of coal and easy access by sea and river. But before that, especially long before that, I thought Swansea and Gower were not important at all.

When I started researching Swansea Castle, I discovered that the Lords of Gower had very important roles in British medieval history. That led to my two popular history books, *Alina, The White Lady of Oystermouth* and *Broken Reed: The Lords of Gower and King John*, which led in turn to *The Magna Carta Story: The Layman's Guide to the Great Charter.*

The area of Gower was known by the Welsh as *Gŵyr*, and was taken soon after 1106 by the Norman Henry de Newburgh (also called Beaumont), Earl of Warwick, with the permission of King Henry I. He anglicized the name and created the Lordship of Gower, which extended inland some way above the Gower peninsular of today, bounded by the River Tawe and the River Llwchwr (Loughor). Henry gave the more fertile areas of land in the lowlands of the peninsular to the English, while the Welsh were relegated to the uplands and the inland part, where the ground was only suitable for grazing sheep.

There was a great wood which stretched across the centre of the land, from Swansea in the east to Loughor in the west. This divided the lordship into *Supraboscus* (above the wood) and *Subboscus* (below the wood). Swansea, then known as Sweynesse or Sweynesey, was built at the lowest crossing-point of the River Tawe, on a high bluff above the river, which provided a natural harbour. The Welsh called it Abertawe, the mouth of the River Tawe. Fabian's Bay to the east was the perfect place for fishing boats to work from, and Oystermouth, at the 'heel' of the peninsular, was where they harvested oysters.

What is now Swansea Bay, a huge sweep of beach which has been likened to the Bay of Naples in Italy, was then farmland, with a bridleway across it, allowing easy access from Swansea to Gower. Indeed, when the tide goes out today, the sea bed is not sand, but mud. There were very few roads, most of Gower was only accessible by boat right up until the 18th century.

So come with me back to medieval times to discover some stories I found when I was researching my books. Some of them have only a tenuous link to Gower, but Gower or the Lord of Gower comes into each of them somewhere.

The same names come up in many of the stories, because the Lords of Gower for much of this time were the de Braose family, whose family tree appears before this introduction. The noble families liked to use the same names for each generation, which makes them difficult to distinguish, so the easiest thing is to number them, as you can see in the family tree. Originally from the village of Briouze-Saint-Gervais in Normandy, the name was anglicised to Braose and later went through other changes, until it ended up as Breos. There are reminders of the family in street names in Swansea today.

1. Gower Fights Back (1136)

Garn Goch Monument

In many minds the Battle of Hastings in 1066 was the conquest of England and therefore the conquest of the British Isles. That's wrong on both counts. The Battle of Hastings put William of Normandy on the English throne, but it took many years to subjugate all of England. Wales, Scotland and Ireland held out even longer. Wales was conquered piecemeal, with incursions by individual Lords to capture lowland areas across the border and along the north and south coasts. These areas were known as the Marches, meaning borderlands.

The Normans gradually took over South Wales as far as Glamorgan, but the Welsh fought back. In 1093 the Normans devastated Gower, and areas further west, but Gower remained 'bloodied but unbowed' until 1099. It was finally taken over by Henry de Newburgh (also called Beaumont) from Brecon, forty miles to the north. To secure it he built several castles, probably of stakes and turf, to house soldiers to keep the people in check: Swansea, Loughor, Llanrhidian and Penrice.

The castles, and others that followed, didn't pacify the Welsh, but were constant reminders of their overlords, and an incentive to continue the fight. The problem for Gower was that the Normans built castles to rule it, and the Welsh rebelled and destroyed everything. The poor peasants probably preferred the Normans, because at least under them the land prospered.

The Welsh used to call themselves Britons and believed not just Wales but the whole of England belonged to them. Young men would rise up and follow any Welsh leader in the hope of restoring the 'British Kingdom'.

The Battle of Garn Goch

In 1136 on New Year's Day, a fierce battle took place on Garngoch Common, which lies between Swansea and Loughor. The ascent of King Stephen to the throne sparked anarchy in England and gave the Welsh an opportunity to recover some of the land taken by the Normans. The Norman knights and men at arms were led by Roger de Newburgh, whose family still held the Lordship of Gower. They had a total of 516 men, many heavily armoured.

The Welsh were led by Hywel ap Maredudd of Brycheiniog (Brecon), and therefore an old enemy of the de Newburghs, who also held Brecon. There were men from Brycheiniog and from North Gower. The Normans set out believing they were facing a small collection of Welsh raiding bands, and were surprised by the scale of the Welsh army. Most of the Welsh were on foot, but managed to surround the Normans. The Welsh attacked mercilessly and gave no quarter - all 516 men were put to the sword, and the bodies left for the wolves.

The Common was named Garngoch after the battle. *Garn* in Welsh means *hilt* as in the handle of a sword, and *goch* means *red*. The Welsh swords were soaked in the blood of their enemies, right up to the hilt. A pile of stones was erected on the common to commemorate this Welsh victory, known as Mynydd Garn Goch - Mountain of Red (or blood) Stones. There is a monument there to this day (see above).

Spurred on by their victory, the Welsh rose in rebellion, and attacked and destroyed many castles, churches and houses and killed people of all ages and ranks. When the King heard of this rebellion, he raised a large force of cavalry and archers, and sent them against the rebels. But the Welsh could not be beaten, killing many of the army, while the rest fled for their lives.

The *Gesta Stephani (Deeds of King Stephen)* records: 'Afterwards the Welsh made a desperate inroad, attended with destruction, far and wide, of churches, vills (towns), corn and cattle, the burning of castles and other fortified places, and the slaughter, dispersion, and sale into captivity in foreign lands of countless numbers, both of the rich and poor.'

Today there is a four-ton stone marking the spot, with two plaques in English and Welsh. After describing the battle the inscription finishes with, 'Land without heritage, land without soul.'

In 1203, King John granted the whole of the lands of Gower to William de Braose, his close friend and ally. The Welsh continued to hold land in Wales, particularly in the mountains where warfare was very difficult, and continued to raid Norman-held territories. It was not until 1284 in the reign of King Edward I that the whole of Wales was finally conquered.

2. The Ogre of Abergavenny (1175)

Abergavenny Castle

Henry Fitzmiles, the third son of Miles of Gloucester, was killed in battle by a Welsh prince, in 1165. The Welsh prince was the Lord of Upper Gwent, Seisyll ap Dyfnwal of Castle Arnallt. He was the brother-in-law of The Lord Rhys.

William II de Braose, the 3rd Lord of Bramber, married Bertha, the second daughter of Miles of Gloucester. Unfortunately all four of Miles' sons died childless so eventually the inheritance was split between his three daughters. The eldest daughter Margaret got the largest share, but William and Bertha got Brecon and Abergavenny to add to their existing Welsh lands. This gave them a vast block of territory in the Middle March of Wales.

Like many Normans, William II was very anti-Welsh, and it caused a lot of trouble. The Welsh were a nuisance because they would not submit. In 1175, William seized the opportunity to avenge the death of his brother-in-law Henry, and caused quite a scandal.

William invited Seisyll, two other princes, and other Welsh leaders of Gwent to Abergavenny Castle. Some historians, including Gerald of Wales, say it was to hear the reading of a royal proclamation, some say it was to a Christmas Day feast of reconciliation. It may have been a combination of the two because the end of the year was a traditional time amongst the Welsh for settling outstanding differences.

Earlier that same year, Seisyll was one of a number of princes of Wales who had incurred the displeasure of King Henry II and travelled to Gloucester to make their peace with him on the feast of Saint James the Apostle (that is 25th July). It was in this spirit of reconciliation that the chieftains of Gwent were invited to attend a feast at Abergavenny Castle, and re-establish amicable relations with their Norman neighbours.

As was the custom, they all left their arms outside the great hall, and went in to the feast. William read the proclamation, which forbade the Welsh from carrying arms. The Welsh leaders were understandably angry at this, and began to shout in protest. William's men had not left their weapons outside the hall, maybe they had hidden them. They rose and murdered all the Welsh, including Seisyll's eldest son Gruffydd who had travelled to the feast with his father. The scene in the hall must have been gruesome indeed.

To make things worse, William's men then made for Seisyll's court at Castle Arnallt. They overwhelmed the guards and entered the castle. Seisyll's wife attempted to escape with her seven-year-old son, Prince Cadwaladr, but they were hunted down and the son was killed in his mother's arms. The men then went on to ravage Seisyll's lands in Gwent.

When William was challenged over the massacre, Gerald of Wales records William's bizarre excuse, that he was tossed into the castle moat and only rescued by his men after the terrible event. William said the men were led by Ranulf Poer, sheriff of Hereford, and it was he who hated the Welsh and seized the opportunity to kill them. Possibly under royal orders, he said, trying to deflect any punishment. Why William's men would throw him in the moat was not explained. Of course Gerald was not the most unbiased source of information regarding these events; he held the office of Archdeacon of Brecon at the time, was well acquainted with both William and his wife and was rather over-lavish in his praise for them.

Whoever was responsible, this resulted in outrage and hostility from the Welsh, whom the kings were always trying to pacify. This action was in violation of all the medieval ideas of hospitality. The killing of Prince Cadwaladr was particularly condemned, as he was only seven years old at the time, and even within the turbulent world of Marcher politics, the killing of children was regarded as reprehensible. The Welsh named William II 'The Ogre of Abergavenny' in honour of his responsibility for the murders.

William was forced to 'retire' from public life for this abuse. He appointed his son, William III, to be in charge of Brecon and Abergavenny. Gerald of Wales emphasised his later piety and generosity to the priories of Abergavenny and Brecon, presumably in an attempt to atone for his crime. William III became a close confidant of King John. In 1203 King John gave him the Lordship of Gower in return for his help in securing the throne. So the son of the Ogre of Abergavenny became the Lord of Gower.

Seven years after the massacre, in 1182, Seisyll's surviving sons attacked the castle and captured many of William's men. William escaped because he was not at home. The sons took their revenge by burning Abergavenny Castle down. The keep survived and William built a new castle.

3. Starved to Death (1210)

King John

King John was considered to be a bad king. His temper was unpredictable, his demands unreasonable and his behaviour appalling. Modern experts who have studied him think he may have been on the autistic spectrum and may have been bipolar, which would explain a lot. The trouble is, back in the 12th and 13th centuries they believed kings were sent by God and had absolute power. Even when the barons later made King John agree to Magna Carta, it didn't make him behave.

It was the third William de Braose who became Lord of Gower as a gift from his close companion King John. John gave him lots of lands and honours. But John was quite paranoid and eventually in 1210 looked at all the lands and power he had given to William and worried about his loyalty. He asked for William's son as a hostage to ensure his faithfulness but William's wife Maud was appalled.

You see, William knew the secret of what happened to John's nephew and contender for the throne, Arthur of Brittany. Everyone suspected but no one knew for sure. When the men arrived to collect her son, Maud said there was no way she would hand over her son to the man who murdered his own nephew. You can imagine the shockwaves! William and his family fled for their lives, first within Wales, then to Ireland.

In Wales they were sheltered by Llywelyn the Great, Prince of Gwynedd, the most powerful man in Wales. This was surprising since Llywelyn was married to King John's daughter Joan (known in Welsh as Siwan), so you would think he would capture them, not hide them from the king. From there they went to Ireland, and then William came back to England and escaped to France through his port of Shoreham, disguised as a beggar. In France William told his secret about the death of Arthur of Brittany, which spread like wildfire, doing yet more damage to King John's reputation.

William's wife Maud and eldest son (the fourth William) were captured in Scotland, having been smuggled there from the north of Ireland. William IV was a grown man with children of his own who were also captured. Many other family members were also rounded up. William's wife Maud and son William were handed over to John, who took a dreadful revenge for her betrayal of his secret.

John had them walled up in a dungeon in Windsor Castle and left them to starve to death. A horror story is told that when the dungeon was eventually opened, William IV was sat upright in a chair with his mother kneeling beside him, embracing him and apparently kissing his cheek. When they looked closer, they found his cheek had been chewed away. He had obviously died first and his mother, starving and in desperation, had chewed his cheek. It was not enough to keep her alive.

Two of William IV's children, John and Giles, were imprisoned at Corfe Castle in Dorset. Two others, Philip and Walter, were held at Angoulême in south-west France. King John's revenge was complete, and they were not released until 1218, two years after King John's death.

4. John de Braose (1202-1232)

Parc le Breos Gardens

In the last story we talked about William IV de Braose and his mother. William's four sons were also locked up by King John. This is the story of William's eldest son John. You would think that John de Braose, whose grandfather was the Lord of Gower and many lands besides, was born into privilege and would have had a comfortable life, but it didn't last long. He was only 12 or 13 in 1210 when his grandfather William III was hounded out of the country by King John, and his grandmother and father, William IV, were walled up in Windsor Castle and left to starve to death.

In his infancy John had been privately nursed by a Welsh woman, in Gower. The Welsh nicknamed him 'Tadody', which means 'fatherless'. They hid him from King John in Gower, and then he was sheltered by his uncle Giles de Braose who was Bishop of Hereford, but in 1214 he was taken into custody along with his brother Giles. I suppose his uncle was too afraid of King John to refuse him once he found out where the boys were.

It's sad to see that King John's revenge reached all the way to the grand-children. John and Giles were put into the custody of Engelard de Cigogny, castellan of Windsor Castle. Their fate was not to be like their father's. They probably lived in some comfort as hostages, but the news of their father and grandparents' fate would have made their captivity distressing.

Engelard was ordered to give the two boys up to William de Harcourt in 1214. But they were not freed, only transferred to Corfe Castle. All this time the barons were getting more and more angry with King John and trying to make him treat people fairly and govern the country properly. It's good to know John de Braose was not forgotten by King John's opponents, as he was present at the signing of the Magna Carta in 1215. But then he went back into captivity.

Peter de Maulay, the constable of Corfe Castle was ordered to free John and Giles into the care of the Bishop of Winchester and Hubert de Burgh in 1216, but they were still not freed. Peter was again ordered to release John and Giles in 1218. This was after King John died, and this time the order seems to have been carried out. The new king was King John's son, Henry III, but he was only 9 years old, so the country was governed by William Marshal as Regent.

William Marshal was an amazing man, probably the greatest knight England ever had, who had served Henry II, Young King Henry, Richard the Lionheart and King John. At a time when men were considered old at 40, he was persuaded to come out of retirement at 70 to lead the country at such a difficult time. William was a very fair and just man, and as Regent he had the power to make people obey, and to undo some of King John's misdeeds.

John's father had been the heir to the de Braose estates and they would in time have come to John as the eldest son. With his father dead and John and his brothers in prison, his uncle Reginald had taken over what lands he could. This left John without any inheritance.

When John was released he was 21, the age of inheritance, and he disputed his uncle Reginald's claim to the Braose lands. Sometimes this came down to actual physical battles. Llywelyn the Great, the most powerful Welshman, helped him to secure Gower in 1219. In return he married Llywelyn's daughter Margaret. In 1221, with the advice and permission of Llewelyn, records tell us he repaired Swansea Castle. He purchased the Rape of Bramber, the original Braose family seat, from his uncle Reginald and his son, another William, in 1226. Sometime in the 1220s, he established the deer park, Parc le Breos (the name mutated over the years) in Gower, which can still be seen today, although the hunting lodge is Victorian and is now a bed and breakfast hotel.

After the death of Reginald in 1228, John became Lord of Skenfrith, Grosmont and Whitecastle, three Marcher castles, by charter from the king but he lost these in 1230 to Hugh de Burgh at the same time as Gower became a subtenancy of de Burgh's Honour of Carmarthen and Cardigan. Once again John suffered loss of his lands.

He had four children: William, Richard, John & Llywelyn de Braose. William was the grandfather of Alina, the subject of my book *Alina, The White Lady of Oystermouth*. John (the father) was killed when he fell from his horse and his foot caught in the stirrup, at Bramber in 1232, and William inherited his estates.

5. The Ensanding of Pennard Castle
(Early 14th century)

Pennard Castle

Pennard Castle in Gower is perched on a limestone spur overlooking the mouth of Pennard Pill stream and Three Cliffs Bay, with a sheer drop below to the north and west. It's a beautiful situation with sweeping views out to sea and across the valley. But the story of the castle is a sad one.

The story is told that a chieftain used to live in Pennard Castle with his warriors. The Prince of Gwynedd, North Wales, asked him for help in a battle with his neighbours and offered him any reward he wanted. The chieftain marched his men north to take part in the battle. The Prince was successful, though the battle was fierce and blood-thirsty.

Afterwards the Prince repeated his offer and asked the chieftain what he wanted as a reward. The chieftain asked the prince for his daughter's hand in marriage, which was granted. To celebrate the victory the chieftain held a great feast in the grounds of the castle, ordering everyone to join in the festivities.

While they were celebrating there was an unusual noise and a sentry reported seeing strange lights along the sands of Three Cliffs Bay. The chieftain was furious that his celebrations were being spoiled. Grabbing his sword and ordering his army to follow, the chieftain raced down from the castle to give battle to the trespassers who had dared to disturb his victory party.

The trespassers turned out to be a group of fairies, dancing around the moonbeams which sparkled along the bay. When the chieftain and his army ran into their party waving their swords, the fairies became angry and called to the chief:

'Stop your warring ways. You cannot harm us with your swords and spears. Cursed shall you and your castle be for spoiling our innocent game!'

The fairies then disappeared and the chieftain and his men became afraid. Looking over the sea, they saw a great sand storm descending from the sky towards them. One dark cloud after another raced up the channel, driving sand through the air. Running for their lives, it was only moments before they all succumbed to the choking sand that roared and tore about them and eroded the masonry.

When the sun next arose, Pennard Castle had become ruined forever in the avalanche of sand which had engulfed it. When the word spread about what had happened it was discovered that a huge mountain of sand had disappeared from a spot in Ireland!

The legend could have a basis in fact, since in 1219 John de Braose, the Lord of Gower, married Margaret, the daughter of Llywelyn the Great, Prince of Gwynedd in the north. John's grandson William married the daughter of Nicholas of Castell Moel, Carmarthen, in 1306. A great sandstorm evidently took place at the beginning of that century, as this William de Braose granted the sandy waste of Pennard to William, his huntsman, showing it was of no further use to him.

Whatever the truth of the matter, the encroachment of the sand was totally unforseen. Pennard Castle and the surrounding village were totally abandoned by the end of the 14th century, and fell into ruin, as had Penmaen Castle over a century before. The last thing to be abandoned was St Mary's Church which was left to the sands in 1532. Restoration work was carried out during the course of the 20th century and the remains of the castle are now protected under UK law as a Grade II* listed building.

6. Llywelyn's Wife (1230)

Llywelyn the Great

The Lords of Gower were Norman and you would think they were enemies of the Welsh, but circumstances often forced them together. Llywelyn the Great was the most powerful Prince in Wales but he made peace with King John and married his daughter Joan. There were also close links between the de Braose barons and Llywelyn's family, even though at times they were enemies. John de Braose, in another story in this book, and Reginald de Braose, John's uncle, were both married to Llywelyn's daughters.

In 1228 William de Braose succeeded his father Reginald, who had been Lord of Gower, and other lands beside. So William was actually Llywelyn's grandson, though it's hard to believe when you look at his behaviour. The Welsh detested him and called him Gwilym Ddu (Black William). During a campaign against Llywelyn the Great, William was fighting alongside another Marcher lord, when he was wounded and captured by Llywelyn near Montgomery. He was held for ransom for £2,000 which was a lot of money in those days, today it would be over a million pounds.

William's wounds were tended by Llywelyn's wife and her maids. He was held for six months, and on his release gave his word he would never again bear arms against Llywelyn, and his daughter Isabel would marry Dafydd, Llywelyn's son and heir.

Not only would this be a third or fourth tie between Llywelyn's family and one of the most prominent Marcher families, but it would bring the Lordship of Builth as a dowry and other potential lands when William died and his lands were split between his four daughters (he had no sons). Even more important, William's wife Eva was the sister of William Marshal, Earl of Pembroke and Regent of England.

While the marriage negotiations were progressing however, there was a major scandal caused by William, father of the potential bride.

At Easter 1230, William visited Llywelyn's court to finalise the marriage arrangements and possibly to negotiate the release of the companions and servants who had been captured with him. One day William was discovered in Llywelyn's chamber in bed with Llywelyn's wife Joan!

It's not known how long the affair had been going on, but it's possible they fell in love when Joan tended William's wounds after he was captured. They were immediately separated and imprisoned. As a Norman Lord, William should have been handed over to the Crown for judgement, but Llywelyn refused to consider it. Within a month William was tried by a council of Llywelyn's lords and sentenced to death. He was hanged publicly on 2 May 1230. Llywelyn, normally the astute politician, behaved as an outraged husband with no regard for the consequences.

Joan was put under house arrest for twelve months, but Llywelyn later forgave her, so it seems there was genuine love between them. But it should be remembered she was also King John's daughter and the half-sister of the present king, Henry III.

There are those historians who say it was a conspiracy to falsely accuse and murder William. Indeed, it did mean his daughters came into their inheritance. But it jeopardised the whole marriage arrangement, so if it was true, Llywelyn was playing a dangerous game. Most likely it was a genuine affair. Llywelyn was at great pains to convince Isabel's relatives the marriage should go ahead.

It's interesting the Crown said nothing about the incident, except a mention in a letter to Llywelyn which referred to the 'mischance that befell him'. There was no mention of the fact he had taken it upon himself to try, judge and execute a subject of the Crown. In fact, he began to style himself 'Prince of Aberffraw and Lord of Snowdon'.

The marriage went ahead and William's lands were split between his four daughters and their husbands.

7. The Little Old Woman of Kidwelly (1242)

Kidwelly Castle

This story is about a noble lady called Hawise de Londres. She is always referred to by her maiden name because she married three times, so her last name kept changing. She was one of the few women who were allowed by the king to hold an inheritance by herself and not have to give it up to her nearest male relative. Her first husband was Walter de Braose, one of the sons of the Lord of Gower, but when this story happened she was a widow for the second time. She lived in Kidwelly Castle and the little old woman of Kidwelly was her friend who helped her in her time of need.

Kidwelly Castle was originally built by the Welsh, captured by the Normans, and taken back by the Welsh. In 1220, Llywelyn the Great restored the castle to the Normans, the de Londres family. The male line of the de Londres had become extinct during these troubles, and Kidwelly passed to an heiress, Hawise.

In 1225 she married Walter de Braose, who died during a campaign in 1233-4 against the Welsh. Walter's father was the Lord of Gower and many lands besides. When his father fell from grace with King John, Walter and his brothers were locked up as hostages. After King John died, they were released and Walter became a significant military figure in South Wales. After Walter's death, Lady Hawise married Henry de Turberville, who died before 1239. Sadly, there were no children from either of these marriages.

This story happened in 1242, when Lady Hawise was again a widow. Later she married Patrick de Chaworth and had three sons and four daughters. When Patrick died in battle, Hawise was granted custody of Kidwelly until her son Payn came of age. She died 5 June 1298 in Kidwelly, and is buried at Ewenny Church, Glamorgan.

This is the story of how Lady Hawise got her castle back from the Welsh.

Every school child in Wales will have heard this nursery rhyme:

Hen fenyw fach Cydweli
Yn gwerthu losin du,
Yn rhifo deg am ddimai
Ond unarddeg i mi.
O dyna'r newydd gorau ddaeth i mi, i mi
Yn rhifo deg am ddimai
Ond unarddeg i mi.

It translates as:

The little old woman of Kidwelly
A seller of sweets is she,
Counts out 10 for a halfpenny
But always 11 for me.
That was very good news for me, for me.
Counts out 10 for a halfpenny
But always 11 for me.

Although she was a Norman, Lady Hawise was sympathetic to her Welsh tenants and unusually for someone in her position spoke fluent Welsh. She had lived in Kidwelly Castle all her life. Welsh rebels led by Meredydd ap Rhys attacked the castle and captured it. At the last minute Lady Hawise escaped down the river Gwendraeth in a small boat leaving her home and everything she owned. Wales was a dangerous place for a Norman lady without protection. Robbers and tramps of all types roamed the land. A Welshman could be executed for minor crimes and taking revenge on the Normans was common practice. Meredydd ap Rhys, for one, had sworn revenge on all Normans and to kill every Norman he saw.

Lady Hawise went to her old friend Angharad the sweet seller. She borrowed some clothes, disguised herself as the old lady, travelled to Dryslwyn Castle and bluffed her way in. Dryslwyn Castle was the home of

Llewelyn the Great. Prince Llewelyn was a Welshman who had married Joan, King John's daughter, and he was Meredydd ap Rhys' lord.

In the great hall Lady Hawise revealed her true identity and pleaded her case. Impressed with her determination and persuaded by his wife, Llewelyn agreed to help Lady Hawise regain Kidwelly Castle. He gave her a parchment with his royal seal commanding Meredith ap Rhys to return the castle to its true owner.

Returning to Kidwelly, Lady Hawise once again needed her disguise to get into the castle. She approached Meredydd as he ate with his men at arms and placed a basket of sweets containing the royal parchment in front of him. Startled he picked up the scroll and broke the seal. As he read Lady Hawise straightened up, cast off the old woman's clothes and spoke loudly in Welsh.

'I am Lady Hawise de Londres. I am Castellan of Kidwelly and I command you to leave and remove your men.'

Meredydd threw aside the royal parchment, leaped up and drew his dagger.

'No man or woman commands me,' he said.

He held the blade to her throat but Lady Hawise did not flinch. Slowly he lowered the dagger.

'Lady Hawise, the decree you bring from Prince Llewelyn is of no consequence to me but your courage cannot be ignored. You shall have your castle. My men and I will be gone within the hour.'

Meredydd ap Rhys kept his word and left Carmarthenshire for ever. Lady Hawise de Londres remained as Castellan of Kidwelly for many years kept company by her Welsh friend Angharad the old sweet lady.

8. The Enemy of my Enemy is my Friend (1320)

Caerphilly Castle

Hugh le Despenser the Younger was King Edward II's favourite, and could persuade him to do almost anything he wanted. In quick succession he secured Gwynllŵg, Usk, Dryslwyn, Cantref Mawr and Emlyn (now known as Newcastle Emlyn). He was known as the most covetous of the Marcher Lords ever. Hugh had obtained the Lordship of Glamorgan, which bordered Gower, by marriage. He wanted Gower, so that the River Loughor would be the border between his lands and the Earl of Lancaster's Lordship of Kidwelly. William de Braose (William VI), Lord of Gower, was short of money so in 1317 he sold Gower to Hugh.

William's daughter Alina was heir to Gower, and her husband John de Mowbray objected to the loss of her inheritance. So when John seized what Hugh had paid for, Hugh persuaded the king to seize it back. John declared that the king's authority did not apply in the Marches, and the other barons agreed. They guarded their Marcher rights jealously and would not allow the king to impose his rule there.

On 26th October 1320, a band of men were sent by the king to take back Swansea Castle for Hugh, but they were met by an armed band of Welshmen in St Thomas who refused to allow them to cross the River Tawe. Why would Welshmen, who hated the Normans, stand up and defend one? Because the king's men were sent on behalf of Hugh le Despenser, and the Welsh hated him above all. So as the ancient proverb says, 'the enemy of my enemy is my friend.'

Llywelyn Bren, or Llywelyn ap Gruffydd, was a Welsh nobleman of Senghenydd, near Caerphilly. He was on excellent terms with Gilbert de Clare, Lord of Glamorgan, holding office under him and acting as the earl's leading adviser on native affairs. He was a man of culture with unusual literary interests for a person of his class and period, possessing considerable property and personal wealth in Senghenydd and Miscin. When de Clare died at the battle of Bannockburn in 1314, it left a power vacuum. The Lordship of Glamorgan passed into royal custody for a while, and the various people who took over Glamorgan treated the Welsh very badly, at a time when they were already suffering a famine.

The latest one was Payn de Turberville of Coity, appointed in 1315, who was no friend of Welshmen, whatever their status, and beat them and extorted money. Llywelyn was removed from office, and insults and accusations went back and forth, which led a furious Llywelyn to tell a room full of his supporters, 'The day will come when I will put an end to the insolence of Payn and give him as good as he gives me.' Eventually Payn charged him with sedition for his support of the oppressed people.

In 1316 Llywelyn appealed to King Edward on their behalf, but the king simply accused him of treason, and ordered him to appear before Parliament. Fearing for his life, he returned home secretly and had no difficulty in raising a widespread revolt among the Welsh hillsmen of Glamorgan. Llywelyn's seven sons took part in the revolt too. The people rose in revolt, attacking Caerphilly Castle on 28th January 1316. Llywelyn and his many supporters - said to number 10,000 - carried off Payn de Turberville's goods into the mountains where they were hiding, and Llywelyn threatened to kill the hated official. This was one of the last serious revolts of the Welsh against their Norman rulers.

The Constable of Caerphilly Castle was captured outside the castle and Llywelyn and his men captured the outer ward but could not break into the inner defences. They burned the town and slaughtered some of its inhabitants and started a siege. The revolt quickly spread through Glamorgan and Gwent; Kenfig castle was sacked, as was the castle at Llantrisant, and several others were attacked, including St Georges-super-

Ely, Llangibby and Dinefwr Castle. Towns were raided and buildings burned, including in Cardiff.

King Edward ordered Humphrey de Bohun, 4th Earl of Hereford and Lord of neighbouring Brecon, to crush the revolt. He gathered overwhelming forces supported by the men of the chief Marcher Lords like Thomas, 2nd Earl of Lancaster and Roger Mortimer. Troops came from Cheshire, North Wales, and also some Welsh soldiers from West Wales. In March, forces advanced from Cardiff and after a battle at Castell Mor Graig they forced Llywelyn and his men to break off the siege of Caerphilly after 6 weeks. The Welsh rebels retreated higher up the north Glamorgan plateau but Humphrey of Hereford and his men were moving south from Brecon.

The forces were so overwhelming that Llewelyn surrendered to Humphrey at Ystradfellte on 18th March 1316, and begged that his followers not be punished, taking all the blame on himself. This earned the respect of Humphrey and Roger, who promised to plead his case with the king. They both urged the king to pardon Llywelyn and it seems likely that their influence won a pardon for many of Llywelyn's men.

However, Llywelyn himself was sent with his family to prison at Brecon on 22nd March. From 27th July 1316 to 17th June 1317 he was held in the Tower of London, but then he became a prisoner of Hugh le Despenser the Younger, the king's favourite, who was lord of many of the lands that had been attacked. Without consulting the king, in 1318 Hugh moved Llywelyn to Cardiff Castle and had him hung, drawn and quartered without a trial. He also imprisoned Llywelyn's wife Lleucu and some of her sons in Cardiff Castle. After the parts of Llywelyn's body were exhibited in various parts of the county he was buried in the Grey Friars at Cardiff. Llywelyn's lands were seized by Hugh. This action was condemned at the time and later used as example of the growing tyranny of Hugh and his father (also called Hugh).

Hugh's treatment of Llywelyn enraged both the Welsh and Marcher Lords, who joined together to petition the king against Hugh, without long-lasting success. When John de Mowbray, the heir to the Lordship of Gower, rebelled against the king, the Welsh supported John because he was fighting Hugh, the most hated of the Normans. The other Lords joined John and the rebellion which followed saw Welsh and Normans fighting together against the king. They managed to free Llywelyn's family and get Hugh and his father exiled, until the king was able to raise a large enough force to counter-attack and put the rebellion down. Humphrey of Hereford took all of Llywelyn's sons into his service around this point.

With the return of the two Hughs to King Edward's court, Lleucu and her sons were again imprisoned, this time in Bristol Castle. However, when Queen Isabella and Roger Mortimer landed in 1326 with an army of mercenaries, the king, unable to command the loyalty of the barons, fled to Hugh's lands in Wales. There they were understandably unable to raise any forces and were captured in November. Hugh suffered the same fate he had inflicted on Llywelyn and was hung, drawn and quartered. One of the charges against him at his trial was the murder of Llywelyn Bren.

With the overthrow of King Edward II, on 11th February 1327 the estates in Senghenydd were restored to Llywelyn Bren's sons - Gruffydd, John, Meurig, Roger, William and Llywelyn. The Earls of Hereford continued to pay at Brecon an allowance to their mother Lleucu until 12th April 1349.

9. Escape from The Tower of London (1323)

The Tower of London

This story links to Gower in two places. William de Braose sold the inheritance of the Lordship of Gower to Baron Roger Mortimer to raise money in 1320. William's daughter Alina and her husband John de Mowbray were supposed to inherit Gower and had even made a contract with William that guaranteed their succession. William actually sold the inheritance of Gower three times over, he was so desperate for money.

Realising the mess he had made, he eventually sold Gower outright to Hugh le Despenser the Younger, the favourite companion of King Edward II. Alina and John saw their Gower inheritance disappearing. John decided to take matters into his own hands, and took control of Swansea Castle. This probably didn't involve force, but taking possession of the official seals. Whatever it took, Hugh was not going to accept it, and persuaded the king to get it back for him.

When the king got involved in the dispute between John and Hugh, the Marcher Lords and other barons who were not happy with the king's favouritism, viewed this action as a challenge to their autonomy, and rose in revolt. Roger Mortimer was one of the barons that joined the rebellion.

Although the barons eventually succeeded in toppling Edward II from the throne, initially the rebellion failed. The leaders of the rebellion were executed, including John de Mowbray, and many of the barons were sent to the Tower of London, including Roger Mortimer. At his trial for treason, Roger was sentenced to life imprisonment. King Edward was sufficiently concerned to appoint a new keeper to the Tower, Stephen de Segrave, in February 1323, and bind him to the tune of £10,000 (over £5 million today) to keep his prisoners safely locked up.

The people were unhappy with the king's weak rule, and more and more were on the side of the barons, so Edward planned to execute Roger, afraid that if he escaped it would have disastrous consequences. The king did not have too long to wait to discover how disastrous, for on the evening of 1st August 1323 Roger Mortimer did indeed escape. Very few people have ever escaped from the Tower, and many of those were caught soon after. But Roger got clean away.

He invited his jailers to dine with him, and his squire drugged their drinks. Roger clearly had friends on the inside and outside. Although the king punished Segrave, Roger had bribed one of his deputies, Gerard de Allspeth, who made a hole in the Tower's kitchen wall so Roger could get out of the building. Allspeth also smuggled in an ingenious rope ladder which Mortimer used to scale the inner and outer wards, to be received by friends outside the walls. When Roger later came into power (see the next story) he pardoned Allspeth for his role in the escape. But to have had men waiting by the Thames suggests a wider conspiracy.

Roger had numerous powerful and important allies, and the key figure seems to have been Bishop Orleton. The king certainly mistrusted the bishop who was relentlessly pursued by royal justice in the following months. Two of Roger's other friends were John de Patesmere, from whom Roger had rented warehouses, and a taverner, Ralph de Boclton.

An inquiry at Portsmouth on 10th August found that Boclton had commandeered a local boat with the help of Alice de Borhunte to row a group of men out to his boat which was at anchor off the coast. Roger made for Portsmouth, and the next day he was on the Continent. He joined his cousins John and Robert de Fienles in Picardy. King Edward wrote them an angry letter on 1st October 1323, in which he expressed his astonishment at their maintenance of Roger on their lands in Picardy. Maybe Roger's mother, Margaret, had appealed to them for help.

His miraculous escape transformed Roger's career. He became *the* focus for opposition to the growing oppression in the country. From his continental base he posed varied threats to the king's position across the

British Isles. Neither Wales nor Ireland could be counted as secure. The king undoubtedly feared Roger and the potential for an invasion.

King Edward was thrown into panic by Roger's escape. He had no idea what the fugitive intended. He was unaware of Roger's flight to France, for his first action was to commission Gruffydd Llwyd and Rhys ap Gruffydd to raise all the forces of Wales to pursue and arrest him. He also ordered the keepers of all ports and the sheriffs of counties in south-east England, as well as the Irish justiciar, to set spies and to inquire whether Roger had crossed the Channel, and who had aided him. On 10th August Hugh le Despenser's father was chosen to head the mission to capture Roger and his adherents.

However, by 26th August information had reached the king that Roger had gone overseas and intended to go to Ireland. Three suspicious Irish ships had been spotted off the Kent coast and spies were set to ascertain their plans. Two days later the authorities of the major Irish towns, the justiciar, and most of the leaders of Anglo-Irish aristocratic society, were ordered to set spies and to pursue and arrest Roger if he came there. Ultimately, Roger made no attempt to go to Ireland. This does not, however, mean that nothing was afoot.

While in France, Queen Isabella met, and fell in love with, Roger Mortimer. Although for different reasons, they were both in opposition to the king, and both believed he was bad for England. They canvassed for support and gathered a growing band of men who were also disenchanted with the king and his administration. They began to raise an army to invade. In September 1326 Isabella and Roger landed in the south of England with 700 mercenaries. The army grew and grew as the disgruntled barons joined their forces to it instead of serving the king. King Edward and Hugh fled but were eventually caught in South Wales.

Edward was locked up and Hugh and his father were tried, convicted and executed. The king agreed to abdicate in favour of his son, if the people would agree to accept him. The abdication was registered on 24th January 1327, and the following day was declared the first day of the reign of Edward III, even though he was only fourteen. Roger and Isabella were appointed as regents. Roger also took the title Earl of March. From prisoner in the Tower to rebel in exile, Roger Mortimer had become effectively the king of England.

10. Has Anyone Seen my Treasure? (1326)

Edward II fleeing to Swansea – plaque designed by 9-year-old boy

King Edward II was a weak king who allowed his favourite male friends to manipulate him and use him to their own advantage. His queen Isabella was from the French royal family and managed to get sent to France to negotiate with the French king, where she was out of the clutches of Edward's favourite Hugh le Despenser the Younger (his father had the same name).

The barons had fought to get the king to behave better but so far he had won. The downfall of the king was sealed when, in September 1326, Queen Isabella and Roger Mortimer landed in the south of England with an army of 700 mercenaries. King Edward was amazed at the small size of their army and immediately attempted to raise a large force to crush them. To his surprise, when he sent messages to call the barons to arms, many of them refused him and many joined the queen. As the army marched north, the invasion quickly had too much support and became too big to stop.

The king and Hugh soon realised they could not prevail against Roger and Isabella. In October they left London and took refuge in Gloucester but the army pursued them. Then they fled to South Wales, where they hoped to mount a defence in Hugh's lands in Gwent and Glamorgan.

When the king fled, he took the great seal of England and a considerable amount of silver with him. Roger was concerned that he would attempt to set up a government in exile. In order to get from Gloucester to Wales, the king went by sea, which was much quicker than by road. While he was at sea, Roger argued that the king had left the country and not appointed a regent, so technically there was no royal authority in England. Roger and Isabella took advantage of this, and appointed fourteen-year-old Prince Edward as regent.

When Edward and Hugh reached Cardiff they were still unable to raise an army, and even their servants deserted them, leaving them with just a few loyal retainers. As they were pursued they fled westward, arriving at Neath Abbey. From there the king sent his treasure, papers and other valuables to Swansea Castle, where he had appointed John de Langton as steward and authorised him to see to the defence of the town.

On 16th November 1326 they were captured in open country on the way to Swansea. Most of their retainers were released, but Hugh and two others were sent to Isabella and Roger at Hereford, tried and executed. The king was taken to the Earl of Lancaster's fortress in the Midlands, Kenilworth Castle. He was persuaded to abdicate in favour of his son, who was crowned King Edward III on 25th January 1327. Roger and Isabella were appointed as regents.

In the upheaval which followed, the valuables were temporarily forgotten; only temporarily however. Five years later, Edward III got rid of the regents and began to rule in his own right. In July 1331, Richard de Peshale in Swansea was commissioned by Edward III to investigate what happened to the king's goods and treasure, which was estimated to be worth £63,000 (about £29m today). It included gold and silver plates, coins and jewellery, fine clothing, arms, armour, horses and of course that 'considerable amount of silver.'

Many of the king's papers were found, but not much else. After three different inquiries about £3000 worth was recovered (about £1.5 million today), and in April 1336 a Royal Commission sought to bring to justice those who had stolen the rest. It does not appear that anyone was convicted. William de Braose, the former Lord of Gower, where Swansea was the administrative centre, was very bad with money and always in debt. Maybe William's debts were paid after all.

If you enjoyed this book, why not leave a review online at Amazon and Goodreads? Reviews are an author's lifeblood.

Available in print and Kindle ebook from Amazon and in multiple ebook formats from Smashwords.com who distribute to major retailers

FREE BOOK!
Join Ann Marie's mailing list and receive this free book and monthly updates
http://eepurl.com/bbOsyz

You might also enjoy the companion books, all illustrated by the same talented artist.

Alina, The White Lady of Oystermouth

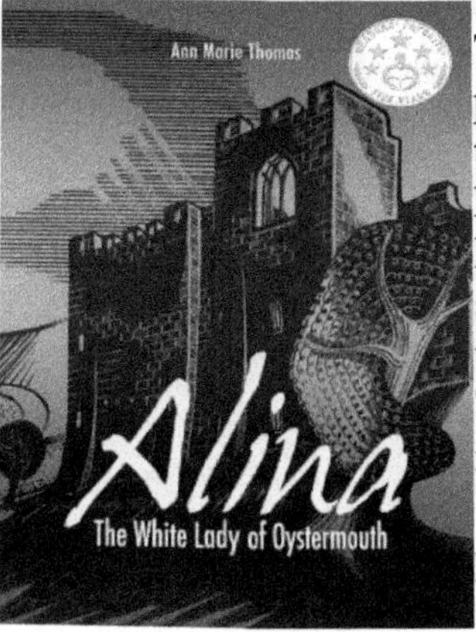

The only book about Alina de Braose and the part that Swansea and Gower played in the toppling of Edward II from the throne. Alina's husband John de Mowbray takes control of the Lordship of Gower in 1320, in an attempt to secure her inheritance. But her father had sold it to the king's favourite, and the king takes it back. The Marcher Barons side with de Mowbray and rebel against the king. But although it eventually leads to the king's downfall, Alina and John will pay a heavy price.
Global link to buy: http://mybook.to/Alina

Broken Reed: The Lords of Gower and King John

The rise and fall of the greatest of the de Braoses, William, 4th Lord of Bramber, Lord of Gower and many other lands besides. Covered in *The Magna Carta Story*, this is the full story from a Gower perspective. It tells the story of how William de Braose rose to a position of great power and influence as a close confidant of King John, but when his wife revealed John's greatest secret John's revenge was brutal. The fall of the de Breos family was the final straw that led to Magna Carta.

Global link to buy: http://mybook.to/BrokenReed

The Magna Carta Story:
The Layman's Guide to the Great Charter

The layman's guide and a good story too. The relationships, arguments, bad behaviour, and civil war around the imposition of the Great Charter on King John, and what happened afterwards. Why is it considered so important after 800 years, and what did it actually say?

Global link to buy:
http://mybook.to/MagnaCartaStory

Swansea Miracle

It was a cold, crisp November morning on Gallows Hill above Swansea Castle. The two convicted men shivered in their thin shirts waiting for the hanging. But this was to be a hanging like no other before or since. One of the men wouldn't stay dead.

Yet another story from medieval Gower, the fascinating series of factual history, told in a storytelling style.

Endorsement

"Welsh history is peppered with forgotten events. Swansea miracle is a gem, a small slice of Swansea History brought beautifully to life and an audience again courtesy of the expert pen of Ann Marie Thomas." Catrin Collier, bestselling Historical Fiction Author

Global link to buy: mybook.to/swanseamiracle

All illustrated by talented artist Carrie Frances.

All available in print and Kindle ebook from Amazon and in multiple ebook formats from Smashwords.com who distribute to all major retailers

www.ingramcontent.com/pod-product-compliance
Lightning Source LLC
Chambersburg PA
CBHW061437050726
47593CB00006B/2376